TALKING JUSTICE:

602 WAYS TO BUILD AND PROMOTE RACIAL HARMONY

by
Tamera Charissé Trotter
and
Joycelyn Racquel Allen

This book is sold with the understanding that the subject matter covered herein is of a general nature and does not constitute legal, accounting or other professional advice for any specific individual or situation. Anyone planning to take action in any of the areas that this book describes should, of course, seek professional advice from accountants, lawyers, tax and other advisers, as would be prudent and advisable under their given circumstances.

R&E Publishers
P.O. Box 2008, Saratoga, CA 95070
Tel: (408) 866-6303   Fax: (408) 866-0825

Book Design and Typesetting by elletro Productions
Book Cover and Illustrations by Kaye Quinn

ISBN 0-88247-982-2

Designed, typeset and totally manufactured in the United States of America.

Lib. of Congress No. 92-50876

DEDICATION

This book is dedicated to
Ms. Marie Duru Chika
and Mrs. Joyce LaVon Allen, our mothers.

Your strength has amazed us,
your courage has impressed us,
your grace inspires us
and your love touches us deeply.

ACKNOWLEDGEMENTS

To our Lord and Savior Jesus Christ
who gives us strength and daily encouragement
to weather the storms of life.

To our families and friends
who are a constant source of support.

We would like to thank the following individuals for their
encouragement:

      Mrs. Cheryl Richardson, Ms. Cathy Vaughn,
      and Mr. Gordon McAlpine.

BEST FRIENDS

Once in a long while, someone walks
    into your life and really makes a
difference.
    They take the time to show you in many ways
that you matter.
    They see and hear the worst in you but do not walk away.
They treasure you and constantly let you know
    what a special blessing from God.... you are!

JOYCELYN AND TAMERA

Introduction

April 29, 1992, the inception of the Los Angeles riots had a tremendous impact on our lives. We will never be the same. And we believe after reading this book, you won't either. Writing this book helped to rekindle and renew the hopes that were devastated over the verdict in an internationally-renowned case. As we awaited the trial's end, we had been hoping that at last justice would prevail. Instead, the justice system failed us, and to many, our lives seemed unvalued by the country we live in. Once again, our country is faced with the task of overcoming racism. We must search within the deep recesses of our hearts and souls to find the

602 Ways to Promote Racial Harmony

answers to questions asked by our younger brothers and sisters. They see their future as an endless struggle against racism and injustice. A future that is bleak and uncertain at best. One in which they are constantly judged based on skin color, economic status, and gender, rather than by merit. We must do all that we can to **stop** the continuum of hate and hopelessness. Therefore, we have channelled our energies in a positive direction. While we too feel the hurt and the rage, we are empowering ourselves through education and awareness. We see the need to provide a tool to aid in the healing process of this nation—a nation crippled by its lack of sensitivity and lack of proactive measures in dealing with racial issues. We are not only promoting cultural awareness but are also providing inspiration and encouragement for families with children. We are offering spiritual direction which quietly echoes our Christian background and strong love for God. We hope that the personal inspiration and optimism this book provides will lay a foundation on which to build and promote racial harmony. We encourage you to celebrate cultural differences rather than fear cultures that are unknown. This book is not an attempt to cover or bury wounds that run very deep. We are not attempting to provide a quick solution, for the road to achieve racial harmony is long and arduous. Yet, the process is simple and everyone has the power to achieve racial harmony. We realize that not all of these thought-provoking, consciousness-raising messages apply to everyone. Use what you can, inspire those who will benefit, and take your first steps to build racial harmony. We see this goal of building racial harmony as the responsibility of every individual. Each one of us has a contribution to make in an effort to reverse the course of events, no matter how small. We must prevent the occurrence of injustice. This can be accomplished through continued cultural education, cultural awareness and cultural understanding. The power to overcome racism is within your reach. And everyone has the means to achieve racial harmony.

The first step begins with you.

602 Ways to Promote Racial Harmony

The fear of cultures that are unknown is probably the most accurate explanation as to why racism exists. We are afraid of what we are unsure of because it is a part of our human nature. However, open and honest dialogue about racial issues increases understanding. Racism builds barriers and creates resentment. Racism separates people on the basis of skin color and prevents a potentially rewarding relationship from occurring.

When you meet someone, do not rely on stereotypes to set the tone. Let your encounters with other races be free of assumptions and do not draw conclusions based on preconceived notions. It is important to not let one negative experience with a certain race define that entire race and create a barrier between the races. You will find shortcomings within every race, but learn to choose your friends based on individual characteristics rather than by what you believe are the tendencies of that race. Racism hurts society because it causes hostility and division rather than unification. There is so much that we stand to learn from each other, now is the time to take advantage of the opportunity to put aside differences and search for commonalties—our humanness.

602 Ways to Promote Racial Harmony

1. **Reach out to everyone, deny no one,
   for we are all members of the human race.**

2. **Don't make assumptions based on stereotypes.**

3. **Acknowledge the contributions
   of people from all cultures.**

4. **Celebrate people.**

5. **Accept cultural differences as being unique,
   not threatening.**

6. **Be comfortable with your own cultural identity.**

7. **Do not try to intimidate
   someone from another race.**

Talking Justice

8. Do not condemn someone's cultural views.

9. Do not condemn someone's cultural traditions.

10. Do not condemn someone's cultural beliefs.

11. Do not perpetrate racism, instead be a voice of justice.

12. Do not pick and choose your friends
    based solely upon their race.

13. Travel outside of your community
    to learn about people that live in other communities.

14. Shop outside of your community.

15. Make friends outside of your community.

602 Ways to Promote Racial Harmony

16. Make friends outside of your culture.

Talking Justice

17. Individuals victimized by racism do not expect differential treatment. They expect fair, unbiased treatment.

18. Justice is ensuring the accordance of all that is fair.

19. Justice does not have to be earned, nor is it a privilege. Justice is a right for all.

20. Read the Bill of Rights, again.

21. Seek justice for everyone.

22. Do not believe everything you read in the newspaper.

23. Do not believe everything you see on television.

602 Ways to Promote Racial Harmony

24. Do not believe everything you hear on the news.

25. Associate freely.

26. Be mindful of the power you have to affect someone's life. It only takes a few moments to alter a person in a negative or positive way.

**27. See a movie
you never imagined yourself seeing.**

28. Read a book you never thought you would read.

29. Allow yourself to experience cultural diversity.

30. Be sincere in your words and deeds.

Talking Justice

31. Do not try to inhibit
    anyone's cultural expression.

32. Be open to the ideas
    of all people.

33. Be less self centered.

34. Experience things
    that you never imagined you would enjoy.

35. If more people thought globally
    and acted locally,
    our nation and world would benefit.

602 Ways to Promote Racial Harmony

36. **Assumptions based on the judgment of someone's race is an injustice.**

37. **Do not make assumptions based on appearance.**

38. **Do not make assumptions based on color.**

39. **Do not make assumptions based on gender.**

40. **All Americans can celebrate June 19th, the anniversary of the Emancipation Proclamation, as another significant "Independence Day" for our country.**

Talking Justice

41. Did you ever notice a salesperson ask to help you first although there was someone in line before you who happened to be a person of color?

42. Admit your own prejudices to yourself.

43. Do not ridicule the language or speech of others.

44. If you see people of color as inferior, do not deny it, change your views.

602 Ways to Promote Racial Harmony

45. When you hear of a crime being committed and you
    assume that a person of color
    has committed it,
    you are making an assumption
    based on a stereotype.

46. Do not deny that you are a racist.

47. Expectations of others should be based on
    someone's ability to meet those expectations.

48. Do not scoff at a person's efforts
    to bring about change.

Talking Justice

**49. Rap music
does not
encourage
or incite violence
in inner city youth.**
It is the poetry and story of their experience.

602 Ways to Promote Racial Harmony

50. Each one of us has a contribution to make
    in an effort to reverse the course of events,
    no matter how small.

51. Do not conform to present racist ideologies.

52. Do not perpetuate negative myths.

53. By keeping silent on racial issues,
    you condone racism,
    discrimination and injustice.

54. Do not make judgments based on unreliable sources.
    Check for facts and proof.

Talking Justice

55. Do not distort facts in order to sway people
to your opinion.

56. Proactionary responses are critical to the
advancement of race relations.

57. Do not encourage people to forget
what has happened in the past.
We must never forget that this nation
was built on the blood and backs of
Native Americans,
African Americans,
Chicanos,
and Asian Americans.

602 Ways to Promote Racial Harmony

**58. Do not build relationships based on fear,
but on objectivity and optimism.**

**59. If you believe that ethnic issues
are not your concern,
then you have an unhealthy
and detrimental attitude
toward race relations.**

**60. Research your political party's stance
on matters regarding ethnic minorities.**

**61. It should not take nationwide violence
to spark awareness of racial issues.**

Talking Justice

62. It should not take nationwide violence
    to spark awareness of socio-economic issues
    in our inner cities.

63. Do not question the need
    for the existence of minority organizations on
    college campuses. They exist to provide support
    and celebrate ethnic cultures.
    They do not espouse separatism.

64. Learn Asian history.

65. Learn Chicano/Latino history.

66. Learn African American history.

602 Ways to Promote Racial Harmony

67. **Learn Native American history.**

68. **Learn and appreciate the histories of all cultures.**

WIGWAM

TEPEE

69. **Do not get upset because Cinco de Mayo, Asian Week, and African American History Month is celebrated each year. European history is celebrated and propagated on a daily basis.**

Talking Justice

70. Celebrate Cinco de Mayo.

71. Celebrate Asian Week.

72. Celebrate African American History Month.

602 Ways to Promote Racial Harmony

73. Learn about the heroes of all cultures.

74. Learn about the heroines of all cultures.

75. Learn about Cesar Chavez.

76. Learn about Rev. Dr. Martin Luther King, Jr.

77. Learn about Malcolm X.

78. Malcolm X was not a violent man.

79. Read the *Autobiography of Malcolm X* by Alex Haley.

80. Malcolm X emphasized aggressive self-defense in an effort to bring about social change.

Talking Justice

81. Be truthful with others,
    if you expect them to be truthful with you.

82. Let your thoughts
    and actions reflect
    the constitutional rights
    that are endowed
    upon every human being.

83. Trust, until you are given a reason not to.

602 Ways to Promote Racial Harmony

84. FORGIVE.

85. Don't sympathize with someone's feelings
and then slander their character
behind closed doors.

86. Question authority.
When authority answers, question it again.

87. Question everything.

88. Never conduct your personal or professional life under a
double standard.

89. Show consistency in your personal
and professional life.

602 Ways to Promote Racial Harmony

90. Be spiritual.

91. Pray for global peace.

92. Change your racist thinking.

93. Respect your elders.

94. Sit next to someone
you have been taught to fear.

95. Treat everyone the same,
regardless of race, or color.

96. Although it will be difficult,
you must admit your prejudice and racist
ideologies before you can deal with them.

Talking Justice

97. Geographical distances
should not stop you
from reaching out to help
in communities that need it.

98. Consider the effect progress will have
seven generations from now. Work to
preserve the national resources we still have.

99. Talk with someone you never imagined shared your
own interests or beliefs.

100. Be aware and concerned about world affairs that may
not affect you directly.

602 Ways to Promote Racial Harmony

101. Don't use race to describe
how a person looks.

102. Be concerned about the issues
that no one will address.

103. Research controversial issues for yourself.

104. Don't use generalizations,
especially on subjects such as:
crimes committed, prison populations,
or welfare recipients.

105. Don't be afraid of people
who are different from you.

Talking Justice

106. **Don't be afraid of people you cannot understand.**

107. **See beauty in people who are different from you.**

108. **Speak up for someone who is different from you.**

109. **If you speak up for someone, then at some point in time, someone will speak up for you.**

602 Ways to Promote Racial Harmony

110. Speak out against racism.

111. Don't speak out on issues that you have not re-
searched nor know concrete facts about.

112. See the good in someone
you thought was an enemy.

113. Meet everyone with a cheerful attitude.

114. Expect everyone you meet
to have a cheerful attitude.

115. Ignorance is not an excuse
for perpetuating racial stereotypes,
thoughts, and actions.

Talking Justice

116. Fear is the inability
     to understand someone
     within their own cultural context.

117. When you look at someone,
     anyone,
     see a person,
     and not a color.

118. When you look at someone,
     anyone,
     see an inner beauty
     rather than an outer appearance.

119. Don't use derogatory words
     to describe how a person looks.

602 Ways to Promote Racial Harmony

120. Don't question
another person's capabilities based on race.

121. Don't discriminate
based on your preconceived assumptions.

122. Don't assume
that athletes are intellectually inferior.

123. Don't judge people by the way they dress.

124. Do not be afraid to politely challenge
     someone who tells prejudicial
     or stereotypical jokes.
     Teach your children to do the same.

125. Racism is learned, not innate.

126. Eating ethnic foods
     does not make you culturally diverse.

127. To eat the foods of other cultures does not mean you
     know and understand their culture.

128. To wear ethnic paraphernalia, to conform to a fad,
     does not mean you understand ethnicity.

602 Ways to Promote Racial Harmony

129. It is true that minorities are owed something:
     equality, parity, and equal representation.

130. When you disregard a person's cultural
     identity, you are denying them their humanity.

131. Reevaluate
     your weaknesses and shortcomings
     in how you relate to those of other races.
     Work on them.

132. All African-Americans do not eat watermelon.

Talking Justice

**133. All African-American males
are not unambitious.**

602 Ways to Promote Racial Harmony

134. **All African-American males
     are not rapists.**

135. **All Chicano/Latinos
     are not lazy.**

136. **All Chicano/Latinos do not
     hold service occupation type jobs.**

137. **All Asians are not superior
     in math and science.**

138. **All Europeans are not racist.**

139. **All Europeans
     are not insensitive to racial issues.**

Talking Justice

140. All African Americans do not think alike.

141. All Chicano/Latinos do not think alike.

142. All Asians do not think alike.

143. All Native Americans do not think alike.

144. All Europeans do not think alike.

145. All African-Americans do not act alike.

146. All Chicano/Latinos do not act alike.

147. All Asians do not act alike.

148. All Native Americans do not act alike.

149. All Europeans do not act alike.

150. Not all people from the inner city are poor.

151. Not all people from the inner city are criminals.

152. Not all people from the inner city are drug dealers.

153. Not all people from the inner city are gang members.

154. Not all drug dealers are African Americans.

155. Not all drug users are African Americans.

Talking Justice

156. Do not close the door on those that try
to help and educate you.
Have an open mind and open heart.

157. Not all African-American males
can play basketball.

158. Not all African-Americans can sing and dance.

159. Criminals come in all colors, shapes, and forms, they
are not exclusive to any one race.

160. There are wrongdoers in all walks of life. This includes
your ethnicity.

602 Ways to Promote Racial Harmony

161. Don't be afraid to ride in the elevator with an African-American or Chicano/Latino male.

162. Do not assume that all African-Americans and Chicano/Latinos in college were admitted through affirmative action.

163. Do not assume that all minorities who work for your company were hired through affirmative action.

164. Not all obese people can sing.

165. Not all obese people are lazy.

166. Not all obese people are incapable of performing certain jobs.

Talking Justice

167. Not all obese people disregard their health.

168. Most minorities are not on welfare.

169. If you are in a position to make a judicial decision, remain objective and unbiased.

170. Assumptions based on race are prejudiced beliefs.

602 Ways to Promote Racial Harmony

171. Understand what racism is
     and what racism means.

172. To deny certain people
     their inalienable rights based upon
     the color of their skin, is racism.

173. Chicano/Latino pride is not racism.

174. To believe that your culture is superior
     to all other cultures, is racism.

175. Asian pride is not racism.

Talking Justice

176. To tell your children to only play with children who are their same color, is racism.

602 Ways to Promote Racial Harmony

177. African American pride is not racism.

178. To believe and act on stereotypes, is racism.

179. Native American pride is not racism.

180. To believe that certain rights are for certain people exclusively, is racism.

181. European pride is not racism.

182. To classify individuals as being ignorant based upon their race, is racism.

183. T-shirts emblazoned
with positive racial slogans
are indicative of racial pride, not racism.

Talking Justice

184. To believe that your culture has a greater aptitude
     than another culture, is racism.

185. To believe that all people
     were not created equally, is racism.

186. To make assumptions based on stereotypes,
     is racism.

187. To assume that someone who is dressed a certain way,
     and is a certain color,
     engages in criminal behaviors, is racism.

602 Ways to Promote Racial Harmony

188. To be a racist is a sign of insecurity.

189. To be a racist is to be ashamed of your own identity.

190. To only allow a certain number of people
     who are of color,
     to enter your place of business at one time,
     is racism.

191. To be a racist is to be afraid.

192. To be a racist is to miss out
     on the true beauty of cultural diversity.

193. To be a racist is to be unaccepting of other cultures.

194. To be a racist is to hurt society.

Talking Justice

195. To be a racist is to be shallow.

196. To be a racist is to be uncertain
of your own importance.

197. To be a racist is to put forth wasted effort.

198. To be a racist is to be a weak-minded person.

199. To experience cultural diversity is unique,
but to understand cultural diversity is profound.

200. To believe that prejudice and bigotry
do not exist in the world is ignorance.

201. Racism is institutionalized.

602 Ways to Promote Racial Harmony

**202. Do not make excuses
for a tradition of racism.**

203. Don't make excuses for ignorance.

204. Racial hatred is ignorance.

**205. To shelter your children during their lives from
experiencing people and places from various walks of
life deprives them of a diverse and rich life.**

**206. When your child questions why someone looks
different, tell them that everyone is unique and
beautiful in their own way.**

**207. Never let your children out of your sight whenever
possible.**

Talking Justice

Children teach us so much every day of our lives. They are innocent at birth and unable to provide for themselves. As children grow and learn, they are either taught to treat others equally, or they are conditioned to believe that equality should not exist for everyone. Their behavior is patterned after their role models and they begin to develop a personality and self-esteem.

You cannot promote racial harmony among other cultures if you discriminate against the obese, the physically challenged, the elderly, and homosexuals. We must teach our children values and principles. It is important to spend quality time with children, teaching them that cultural differences are unique. We should teach them to be proud of their identity and to be accepting of people who are different from them. We should not condition children to hate, but to be open to the ideas of all people.

602 Ways to Promote Racial Harmony

**208. Make friends
with your parents.**

**209. Make friends
with your children.**

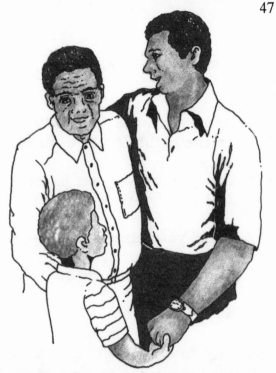

602 Ways to Promote Racial Harmony

210. Don't compare your children
     to the children of your friends.

211. Don't compare your parents
     to the parents of your friends.

212. Raise your children to see with their hearts.

213. Raise your children to judge with their hearts.

214. Expose your children to all cultures.

215. Buy your child dolls from all ethnicities.

Talking Justice

216. **Be careful of what you say
in the presence of your children.
How they act, react, and treat others
is a reflection of you.**

217. **Teach your children that a true democracy will have
equal representation from all races, ethnicities, and
genders, in all levels of society.**

602 Ways to Promote Racial Harmony

218. Inspire your children in whatever their endeavors.

219. Motivate your children to be achievers at an early age.

220. Respect your parents, for their wisdom is invaluable.

221. Respect your children, for their ideas represent the future.

222. Respect your teachers, for their lessons can be applied to all areas of your life.

Talking Justice

We can empower ourselves to end racism through massive education. Unfortunately, few people pursue the many arenas available in which they can learn about other cultures. Sadly many people use their televisions as a school for themselves and their children.

The media has defined images for you which only serve to exacerbate the problem of racism. We encourage you to take advantage of books and people to teach you about other cultures. Empowerment comes through education. If you remain ignorant and blind to the critical issues of race and humanity, you will have no power to influence positive change.

602 Ways to Promote Racial Harmony

223. Monitor
    the television shows
    that your children watch,
    and limit their television viewing.

602 Ways to Promote Racial Harmony

224. Take an active role
in your children's education.

225. Help your children with their homework.

226. When your children speak, listen.

227. When your children stop speaking, know.

228. Allow your children
to make their own mistakes.

229. Show your children
that you are proud of them.

230. Tell your children
that you are proud of them.

Talking Justice

231. Don't always discipline with a spanking.
     Learn behavior modification.

232. Encouragement often works better
     than criticism.

233. Allow your children
     to make their own career choice.

234. Support
     the career choices
     your children make.

235. Downplay your weaknesses,
     and highlight your strengths.

236. Turn your liabilities into assets.

602 Ways to Promote Racial Harmony

237. Always care enough to tell your children the truth.

238. Always care enough to tell your parents the truth.

239. Always be willing to give your children another chance.

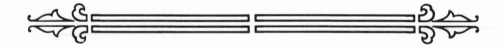

240. Always be willing to give your parents another chance.

241. Parents, discuss your expectations with your children.

Talking Justice

242. Children, discuss your expectations with your parents.

243. Husband,
     communicate your expectations with your wife.

244. Wife, communicate your expectations
     with your husband.

245. Parents, if you cannot live up
     to the expectations of your children, tell them.

246. Children, if you cannot live up to the expectations of
     your parents, tell them.

247. Husband, if you cannot live up to the expectations of
     your wife, tell her.

602 Ways to Promote Racial Harmony

248. Wife, if you cannot live up to the expectations of your husband, tell him.

249. If you nurture your relationships
     they will remain vibrant and alive.

250. If you set boundaries
     in your relationships,
     they will become lasting friendships.

251. In your relationships at home,
     and in the workplace,
     learn to compromise.

Talking Justice

252. COMPROMISE.

602 Ways to Promote Racial Harmony

253. **Educate your children on health, sex, and drug issues. Answer their questions openly.**

254. **Do not allow someone else to discipline your child.**

255. **Accept the fact that you have been taught racist ideology through the media, the educational system, and society as a whole.**

256. **You have the power to curb racial stereotyping in your neighborhoods, and you can begin at your front door.**

257. **Read, *"I Dream A World"*, by Brian Lanker. The strength and courage of the women featured will inspire you.**

Talking Justice

258. Do not fault your children
     if they make racist statements.
     Teach them to appreciate other cultures
     and expose them to other cultures.

259. As your knowledge and awareness
     of racial issues increase,
     your capacity for understanding
     will also increase.

260. Do not force your children
     to conform to your racist ideologies.

261. Stop being complacent and become assertive
     in your attempt to improve race relations.

602 Ways to Promote Racial Harmony

**262. Translate your positive thoughts
into positive actions.**

**263. Racism is perpetuated
in the judicial system
when blatant evidence is brought
before the court,
yet a fair verdict is not rendered.**

Talking Justice

264. When those who are charged
to "protect and serve,"
are treated as though
they are above the law,
that is injustice.

265. When the life of an animal
is priced higher than the life
of a human being,
that's injustice.

266. Support your children,
family, and friends
in their efforts to gain knowledge
and become enlightened
on racial issues.

602 Ways to Promote Racial Harmony

267. Vote for the most qualified candidate.

Talking Justice

268. Be more appreciative.

269. Be more understanding.

270. Be more empathetic.

**271. Allow these three things
to propel you into action.**

272. Hire the most qualified applicant.

602 Ways to Promote Racial Harmony

273. Women working in the same capacity as a man not only deserve equal pay, they are entitled to equal pay.

274. Pray for peace among all people.

275. Never underestimate the power of God.

276. Employers give raises.

277. Employees always perform above excellence and beyond your job description.

Talking Justice

278. Don't yell at your children.

279. Don't yell at your parents.

280. Don't yell at your wife.

281. Don't yell at your husband.

282. Don't be too quick to criticize.

283. People
    who are
    homeless
    need assistance,
    do not blame them.
    Many of them are innocent children.

602 Ways to Promote Racial Harmony

284. Visit historical monuments.

Talking Justice

285. Volunteer to work
     at inner city community centers,
     they are always understaffed and underfunded.

286. Listen and learn from the wisdom of others.

287. Encourage everyone you know to vote.

288. Become active on a political committee
     or campaign that works to insure parity
     and equality for all people.

289. Listen to youth.

290. If your child is a homosexual,
     accept him for who he is,
     not what he is.

602 Ways to Promote Racial Harmony

291. **If you have grandchildren
    as a result of an interracial relationship,
    accept and love them as part of your family.
    Do not withhold your love from them.**

292. **If your child is involved in an interracial
    relationship, be supportive, not judgmental.**

293. **African American people are beautiful.**

294. **Asian people are beautiful.**

295. **Chicano/Latino people are beautiful.**

296. **Native American people are beautiful.**

297. **European people are beautiful.**

Talking Justice

298. All of God's children are beautiful.

602 Ways to Promote Racial Harmony

299. If you think that most people on welfare,
     want to be, you are wrong.

300. If you think most people on welfare are
     African Americans, you are wrong.

301. If you think that our nation does not have serious
     problems, in regards to race relations, you are wrong.

302. Overcome your fears by learning not to
     prejudge. Give everyone the chance to
     brighten your life.

Talking Justice

The benefits of becoming culturally well-rounded are too numerous to note. However, we encourage you to consider that the advantages far outweigh the disadvantages. Perhaps one of the greatest benefits is that the possibility of living in a society not fueled by hate but by compassion and equality will become more probable as you work to fight racism.

The price we have paid for racism is deep division and widespread disenfranchisement. There are many invisible walls that continue to divide and separate us from achieving racial harmony. We must tear down these barriers that perpetuate fear and ignorance.

602 Ways to Promote Racial Harmony

303. Do more.

304. Expect less in return.

305. Read more.

306. Talk less.

307. Listen more.

308. Increase your optimism.

309. Be more flexible.

602 Ways to Promote Racial Harmony

310. **Learn to adapt more
to unusual situations and experiences.**

311. **Pay less attention to what people say
and more to what they do.**

312. **The capacity for change is great
no matter how old you are.**

313. **It is never too late to change the course
of events.**

314. **Do not give in to peer pressure
and emulate those with racist tendencies.**

Talking Justice

315. **Stimulate discussion with those around you to increase your knowledge on issues of critical importance.**

316. **Engage your children in activities that foster wholesome attitudes toward all people.**

317. **Do not abuse your spouse.**

318. **Do not abuse your children.**

319. **Seek counseling if you are an abuser. Do not let your behavior cause irreparable damage to your family.**

320. **Develop your interpersonal relationships.**

602 Ways to Promote Racial Harmony

321. No matter what the circumstance, turn to God.

322. No matter what the circumstance, rely on God.

323. Listen to the voices that speak through literature and the arts. They can help you understand other cultures.

324. Teach the Bible to your children.

325. Teach your children about cultural differences, and teach them to appreciate other cultures.

326. The efforts you put forth to build racial harmony will manifest in small ways.

Talking Justice

327. Maintain a positive outlook
in the midst of negativism.

328. A nation that continually spends
more money in support of other countries
rather than investing in its own people
has its priorities misaligned.

329. Do not pass value judgments based on race, dress,
size, religion, or sex.

330. Do not use abusive language around your children.

331. Do not patronize or condescend
to someone of another race.

602 Ways to Promote Racial Harmony

332. Do not look down on those who work
in service occupations.

333. When you compromise your morals for instant gratification, you jeopardize future success.

334. Respect an individual's right to choose a marriage
partner.

335. The best way to change the system is from the inside.
Tragically, too many of us are forced to be outside
observers, powerless and voiceless.

336. Do not engage in conservations with people
who slander other races.

337. Encourage others to stop slandering other races.

Talking Justice

338. Don't vote along party lines simply because you have been conditioned to do so.

339. Know your local elected officials by name and stay informed on local issues. Remember, they work for you.

340. As long as job opportunities, adequate, affordable housing, and education remain second priority, we are far from being a secure, sound nation.

341. Be professional in all aspects of your life.

342. It takes the strength of your character to accept that you are a racist, and a strong will to make a change.

602 Ways to Promote Racial Harmony

343. All things are possible, even the improbable.

344. The more you practice it,
   the more permanence you will have
   in achieving racial harmony.

345. Improving race relations begins with small measures of
   kindness and courtesy.

346. Observe more.

347. Be cognizant of the things
   going on around you.

348. Do not assimilate.

349. Pessimism and cynicism deter progress.

Talking Justice

350. Do not reject someone's solutions
unless you can provide your own.

351. Learn to accept some things as they are.

352. The roots of racism are deep,
but they can be uprooted.

353. If you think that the problems with race relations were
caused solely by minorities, you are wrong.

354. Learn to cherish silence. Your spirit speaks most
loudly at these times.

602 Ways to Promote Racial Harmony

355. Learn to cherish solitude. Being alone every now and then aids in your growth and development. It also allows you to see things with unobstructed vision.

356. Learn to challenge certain patterns of thought that have controlled your behavior.

357. Equality does not mean that ethnic minorities want the right to assimilate into American society.

358. Spend more time fighting injustice rather than fighting to keep racism alive.

359. Think about what you say before you say it. Words have as much of a capacity to inflict pain as does physical violence.

Talking Justice

360. **Do not submit to peer pressure.**
     Do not betray yourself.

361. **Do not regard your family as an entity unto itself; but**
     as part and parcel of a larger community filled with all
     races, creeds and colors of people.

362. **As long as elite organizations have a**
     closed door policy in regards to minority
     membership, racial harmony will never
     be achieved in our country.

363. **In order for ethnic minorities to transcend**
     the limitations of race, those people in power need to
     remove those limitations from in front of them. Any
     limitations placed on a people impedes the progress of
     the people.

602 Ways to Promote Racial Harmony

364. We are a nation unaware of our true promise
and potential. This ignorance can prove to be
more devastating than any nuclear fallout.

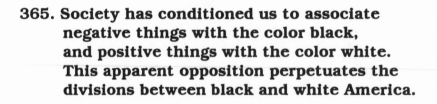

365. Society has conditioned us to associate
negative things with the color black,
and positive things with the color white.
This apparent opposition perpetuates the
divisions between black and white America.

366. The large gap between the incomes of
white men versus African American men, and white
women versus African American women perpetuate
racism and sexism in the workplace.

Talking Justice

367. The gap in the percentage of mortgage loans awarded to whites versus African Americans perpetuates racism in the banking industry.

602 Ways to Promote Racial Harmony

368. Falsifying information about home rentals and availability to prospective clients perpetuates racism in the housing and real estate industries.

369. Racism is perpetuated in the auto industry when car prices or down payments are increased for ethnic minorities.

370. Placing a glass ceiling on an ethnic minority perpetuates racism in the workplace.

371. Neglecting to help a customer in a store because of their ethnic makeup perpetuates racism in the retail industry.

372. I.Q. tests are biased scales that perpetuate racism because they are written from only one frame of reference.

Talking Justice

373. Treating a student of ethnic origin as if he cannot perform to basic standards perpetuates racism in the educational system.

374. Not awarding major film roles to ethnic minorities based on race perpetuates racism in the film industry.

375. Not awarding major film roles to people based on gender perpetuates discrimination in the film industry.

376. Do not teach your children that a person with blond hair and blue eyes is the epitome of beauty. There is a range of beauty from alabaster to ebony.

377. If you are interested in raising children, consider adoption.

602 Ways to Promote Racial Harmony

378. If you think that African Americans should move to Africa, that is a racist thought.

379. Covert racism is the most detrimental to society, because the victims do not know who are their racist enemies.

380. Do not use racial terms or tell racist jokes.

381. If an ethnic minority moves into your neighborhood and you begin to panic, you may be a racist.

382. The best way to get to know ethnic people is to interact and communicate with them.

383. Your ability to communicate with ethnic minorities will increase with continuous interaction.

Talking Justice

384. As you achieve your life goals,
help someone less fortunate than you
to reach their goals.

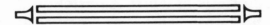

385. The potential for greatness in the nation will not be
met until there is a priority placed on improving race
relations.

386. If you think ethnic minorities are not as intelligent as
you, you are a racist.

387. If you have harmony within yourself,
it will radiate to others.

602 Ways to Promote Racial Harmony

388. Become more comfortable
      about discussing issues of race.

389. Ethnic minorities are forced to meet
      the expectations of white America
      in both their professional and personal lives.

390. The impact of racism
      has perhaps been most detrimental to the
      African-American male.

391. If you must judge African-American males,
      judge each African-American male on an
      individual basis, rather than on a collective basis.
      Let them succeed,
      or fail on their own individual merit.

Talking Justice

392. Read the eyes of young African-American men.
Behind them lie deep rivers of hurt,
anger, disappointment, and confusion.

393. Why are African-American men usually portrayed
by the mass media as if they are chief villains?

394. The white male must acknowledge
that his African-American male counterpart
is capable of achieving upward mobility,
if given an equal opportunity to do so.

395. The African-American male
is an endangered species due to the fact
that they top the lists of the six leading causes
of death of the adult population— homicide, cancer,
strokes, heart attacks, suicide, and accidents.

396. Do not mimic the traditions of ethnic people.
Respect and celebrate their traditions.

397. One minority does not speak for, nor represent,
an entire race.

398. To travel the world without seeing what is in
your own backyard, is to not know the world at all.

399. Make the best of what you have,
and build on it from there.

400. Inner-city schools should have educational tools and
resources comparable to those of suburban schools.

401. Be able to laugh at yourself.

Talking Justice

402. Encourage our political leaders
     to decrease nuclear arms spending
     and increase spending on health care,
     housing, education, and employment.

403. Research all political candidates before voting.

404. Know your congressmen.

405. Write to your congressmen.

406. Complain to your congressmen.

602 Ways to Promote Racial Harmony

407. Realize that AIDS is an epidemic that affects all ages, colors, communities, and people.

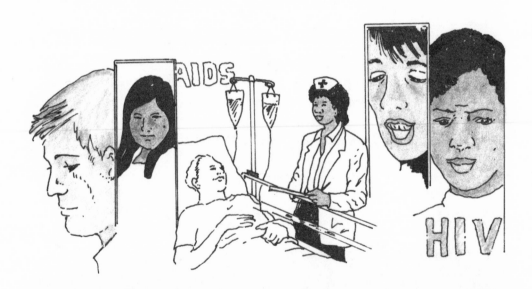

Talking Justice

408. Help prevent the spread of AIDS, practice safe sex!

409. Do not alienate people with AIDS.

410. Earn everything.

411. Learn to read.

412. Learn to write.

413. Finish school.

602 Ways to Promote Racial Harmony

414. Meditate daily.

415. Be proud of the person God made you to be.

416. Pray often.

417. Give someone a hug who is in need.

418. Seek the guidance of your elders.

419. Approach each encounter with someone with enthusiasm.

420. Love unconditionally and across all racial lines.

421. Give unconditionally and across all racial lines.

422. Above all, be honest.

Talking Justice

423. **Treat all of your employees fairly and they will perform to the best of their abilities.**

424. **Do not expose your employees to chemicals and pesticides that endanger their health.**

425. **Companies that dump chemical waste in minority communities practice environmental racism.**

426. **Donate money to a worthy cause.**

427. **Donate your time to causes that promote social progress.**

428. **Listen to the words of songs and hear their messages.**

429. **Respect the physically challenged.**

602 Ways to Promote Racial Harmony

430. **Make decisions**
     based on your own experiences and intuition.

431. **Trust your first instinct.**
     Sometimes it is your best instinct.

432. **Strive for racial harmony within your life, and**
     perhaps it will spread throughout the lives of others.

433. **First impressions are not always accurate.**

Talking Justice

434. Use your negative experiences as stepping stones to positive growth.

435. Take the time to tell someone you care and do this often.

436. Do your part to help keep the earth environmentally safe.

437. See the movie *"Imitation of Life"*.

438. See *"Roots"*.

439. Acknowledge that homosexuals are human beings and treat them as such.

602 Ways to Promote Racial Harmony

440. Accept interracial relationships.

Talking Justice

441. Accept interracial marriages.

442. Always treat your customers with dignity and respect.

443. Greet all of your customers with a "Hello" or "How are you?" and mean it.

444. Do not insult a customer who asks "How much is it?" by replying, "It's really expensive."

445. Empower yourself through education and awareness to achieve your life's goals.

446. Attain peace of mind.

447. Do not make fun at the expense of others.

602 Ways to Promote Racial Harmony

448. Do not settle for mediocrity in any area of your life.

449. Each day, plant a seed for the harvest
of racial harmony. Cultivate your garden.

450. Resolve your racist encounters
and replace them with new friendships.

451. Take time to write letters of complaint
protesting racist activities.

452. If you experience a racist encounter with someone,
do not assume that all members of that race
are the same.

453. Understand affirmative action.

Talking Justice

454. Never have expectations of others that are based on stereotypes.

455. Look out for the safety of your neighbor's children.

456. Investigate our political leaders' real agendas.

457. Maintain control of your thoughts. You will be able to think clearly in unusual situations.

602 Ways to Promote Racial Harmony

458. Maintain control of your actions. You will be able to act rationally in unusual situations.

459. Cooperate with those who try to make reforms in the best interest of the people.

460. Perseverance is necessary to make long term change and progress.

461. Mobilize your community to act positively to improve race relations.

462. Do not let your actions be governed by guilt, but by a true desire to bring about change.

463. Do not be too proud to admit your past mistakes.

Talking Justice

464. Allow those with knowledge to teach you.

465. Do not allow someone else to thwart your efforts.

466. If you stand up for others, others will stand up for you.

467. We are all endowed with the capacity for human understanding.

468. Rather than be defensive, be on the offensive to work to achieve racial harmony.

469. To overcome the obstacles present in a racist society, we must be willing to jump the hurdles.

602 Ways to Promote Racial Harmony

470.

Education

+

Hope

+

Understanding

+

Action

=

Progress.

Talking Justice

471. Do not patronize someone by altering your language so it sounds like theirs.

472. Do not feel that you must isolate your family from other cultures in order to protect them.

473. Do not use hostility to set the tone in dealing with ethnic minorities. This only exacerbates the situation.

474. Help create opportunities geared towards improving someone's quality of life.

475. You will not understand the current state of affairs in minority communities until you first understand critical past events. Learn the history of all cultures.

602 Ways to Promote Racial Harmony

476. Be a racial harmony role model for your children, neighborhood, and workplace.

477. Do not be offended if someone confronts you about an insensitive comment. Take it as constructive criticism.

478. Make suggestions to our policy makers on how they can make legislative changes to fight discrimination.

479. Make conscious choices. The choices you make today will set the tone for tomorrow's events.

480. Learning how to achieve racial harmony is a continuous process.

Talking Justice

481. Do what you can to ease racial tensions
in your community.

482. Resolve the contradictions in your life.

483. Change your ambivalent feelings to caring feelings.

484. If you prejudge someone, you will miss out
on a potentially rewarding encounter.

485. It takes a courageous person
to confront racial adversaries. Be courageous.

486. It takes a person with integrity to be true to herself.
Be honorable.

487. It takes a person with understanding
     to know how the past
     has affected the present
     in regards to racial issues.
     Be understanding.

488. It takes a compassionate person to share the pain
     caused by racism. Be compassionate.

489. It takes a patient person to realize
     that the process of growth is slow. Have patience.

490. It takes a person with tolerance
     to deal with the ebb and flow. Be tolerant.

491. It takes a person with determination
     to break racist habits. Be steadfast.

Talking Justice

492. As long as people think only of themselves
and have no compassion for others,
there will be no racial harmony.

493. When people show compassion and make an effort
to learn about others, there can be racial harmony.

494. As long as individuals act on stereotypes,
there will be no racial harmony.

495. When parents teach their children
to value and respect all people,
there will be racial harmony.

602 Ways to Promote Racial Harmony

496. As long as organizations formed to promote
     racial hatred continue to function,
     there will be no racial harmony.

497. As long as people who live in the suburbs feel no com-
     monality with the people who live in the inner city,
     there will be no racial harmony.

498. As long as any one race considers itself to be the supe-
     rior race, and acts upon these beliefs, there will be no
     racial harmony.

499. When people celebrate cultural differences and appre-
     ciate all cultures, there can be racial harmony.

500. As long as the justice system is unjust and racially
     biased, there will be no racial harmony.

Talking Justice

501. When our justice system
applies equal justice to all people,
there can be racial harmony.

502. If you constantly make derogatory remarks centered
around someone's race, you may be a racist.

503. Do you believe that ethnic minorities should only
perform subservient duties? If so, you may be a racist.

504. If you show through your actions and reactions that
you have biased feelings towards people of color, you
are probably a racist.

505. Subtle racism echoes loud and clear.

602 Ways to Promote Racial Harmony

506. If you feel uncomfortable
with someone of color
entering your home,
you may have
racist tendencies.

Talking Justice

507. Listen to Rev. Dr. Martin Luther King Jr.'s speech,
     "I Have A Dream."

508. In order to build racial harmony, you must first bridge
     gaps between yourself and other cultures.

509. In order to build racial harmony,
     you must first break traditions.

510. In order to build racial harmony,
     you must be willing to commit to make change.

511. If your children make racist comments
     in your presence and you do not reprimand them,
     you are condoning racism
     and setting a poor example for your children.

602 Ways to Promote Racial Harmony

512. Do not use racism
     as a false front to cause controversy.

513. It takes an honest person to confront a friend
     who may be a racist. Be true to your friends.

514. As you journey toward racial harmony within your life,
     bring along a friend.

515. You have the power to make changes within your life.

516. If you believe that God created all people equally,
     but you say that people of color are inferior,
     you are living under a double standard.

Talking Justice

517. Racism is a disease of epidemic proportions,
and if it remains unchecked,
will continue to have catastrophic effects
on our nation.

518. The discrimination against Native Americans in the
1600's is something that too many of us have forgotten.

519. The discrimination against Native Americans now
is something that too many of us ignore.

520. When people protest about something they feel is
racist, do not disregard them. Listen to their issues.

521. Antidiscrimination laws need to be enforced to their
fullest extent before true parity can be achieved.

602 Ways to Promote Racial Harmony

522. Minority entrepreneurs need more support
and we should be committed to their success.

523. African Americans comprise twelve percent
of the nation's population, but represent twenty
percent of the unemployed.
An increase in job opportunities is needed
in order for this to improve.

524. Concerned individuals should ask each other if they
exhibit positive role model behavior to children.

525. Human relationships have disintegrated
due to the advancement of modern technology.
Human beings should be valued more than machines.

Talking Justice

526. Do not be afraid of the word revolution.
It merely means that necessary changes are imminent
in order to achieve a balance in opportunity.

527. Live your life based on interdependent thinking
and collective action.

528. There can be no world solidarity
until we have national and cultural solidarity.

529. Do not let misunderstanding and malice
rule your actions.

530. Work actively in an organization that was formed
to eliminate the injustice that has been perpetuated
on ethnic people.

602 Ways to Promote Racial Harmony

531. When physical or emotional violence
is perpetrated upon a people, it becomes necessary
to defend oneself against the aggressor.

532. Make sure that you leave a fertile land for our next
generation to cultivate in the way of race relations.

533. The children are our future.
Mold and shape them to be gentle spirits.

534. In order to build racial harmony,
you must first let racial harmony
manifest itself within your own life,
be an example for others,
and be committed to pass it on.

Talking Justice

535. Do not teach your children
to deny the reality of our nation.

536. Acquire insight into your own existence. This
knowledge may help you understand other cultures.

537. White supremacy should be viewed
as a calculated attack against all ethnic minorities.

538. African-Americans will continue to be
disproportionately represented in the criminal justice
system as long as the gaps in socioeconomic status
between cultural groups are allowed to widen.

539. Many political leaders
project a false image of their true selves.

602 Ways to Promote Racial Harmony

540. The morbidity and mortality rates for
     African-American babies is atrociously high
     due to the lack of access to adequate prenatal care.

541. In order for our nation to truly serve all ethnic people,
     the justice system needs a complete overhaul.

542. Adequate support systems need to be put into place to
     encourage the development of young minds.

543. As we move into the 21st century as a nation, it is
     imperative that we develop a nation with a set of
     principles geared to benefit all people.

544. A racist culture produces racist minds.

Talking Justice

545. A sexist culture produces sexist minds.

546. A hate-filled culture produces hate-filled minds.

547. An ignorant culture produces ignorant minds.

548. A homophobic culture produces homophobic minds.

549. An uneducated culture produces uneducated minds.

550. A passive culture produces passive minds.

551. A culture influenced by biased media
produces minds influenced by biased media.

552. A materialistic, value-displaced culture
produces materialistic, value-displaced minds.

602 Ways to Promote Racial Harmony

553. An ideal society is one where individuals are not
oppressed because of race, religion, gender
or sexual preference.

554. Showing pride for your own ethnicity does not mean
you are being disrespectful to another ethnicity.

555. When handling a racist encounter,
opt to educate, rather than defend.

556. If you believe that racism does not occur
on a daily basis, you are denying reality.

557. A racist phrase you have used for years
keeps the tide of racism flowing.

Talking Justice

558. The racial hatred you have passed from one generation
to the next allows racism to flourish.
Change now for our future generations.

559. Do not waste your life being a racist.
Life is much too short.

560. The person who saves your life
could be someone you have been taught to hate.

561. If you believe that God is love,
but you cannot love all people,
then you are living in contradiction of your beliefs.

562. Although many of us have been hurt,
we can all be healed.

602 Ways to Promote Racial Harmony

563. In order to improve race relations, people from all levels and industries in society must be committed to achieve this common goal.

564. In order to understand others within their own cultural context, you must learn about the terms that they use to define themselves.

565. Achieving racial harmony can add the sense of inner peace that you have been searching for.

566. Achieving racial harmony should be among your top ten priorities.

567. As long as race discrimination exists in the workplace and job opportunities remain unequal, there will be no racial harmony.

Talking Justice

568. When individuals are judged on their own merits,
there can be racial harmony.

569. As long as the judicial system
continues to discriminate based on race,
there will be no racial harmony.

570. When all races believe that all people are equal,
there can be racial harmony.

571. When people stop acting and reacting
based on stereotypes, there can be racial harmony.

572. As long as people are judged by the color of their skin,
there will be no racial harmony.

602 Ways to Promote Racial Harmony

573. As long as parents raise their children to segregate
themselves from children of other races,
there will be no racial harmony.

574. When people respect all people regardless of race,
there can be racial harmony.

575. As long as those individuals charged to protect
and serve are treated above the law,
there will be no racial harmony.

576. As long as those individuals who are racist deny they
are racist, there will be no racial harmony.

577. As long as family traditions of racism continue,
the vicious cycle will continue, and there will be no
racial harmony.

Talking Justice

578. Do not give up your quest to achieve racial harmony.

579. A courageous person defies all odds
and endures until the end.

580. Have courage.

581. The person willing to admit his faults
and determined to make a positive change,
is the one who will be rewarded.

582. When people value people,
there can be racial harmony.

583. Look beyond color.

602 Ways to Promote Racial Harmony

584. Look beyond race.

585. Look beyond stereotypes.

586. Look beyond unrooted assumptions.

587. Look beyond your supremacist thoughts.

588. Look beyond your own culture and realize that other people's cultures have as much value as yours.

589. Look beyond the misconceptions.

590. Look beyond the ignorance.

591. Look beyond the hate.

Talking Justice

592. Envision peace among all people.

602 Ways to Promote Racial Harmony

593. Look to the power of God and find healing.

594. Look beyond your negative judgments of others
and see positive possibilities.

595. Look beyond your own little world
and learn to see and relate to the world of others.

596. Look beyond your own egotism
and seek the wisdom of others.

597. Look beyond your ability to first pass judgment
and realize that you may not always be right.

598. Be concerned about the welfare of others.

Talking Justice

599. Each day need not be a struggle with racism.

601. The task to counter racism is large,
but not insurmountable.

602. The potential for racial harmony is great.
The first real steps begin with you.

602 Ways to Promote Racial Harmony